Navajo Weavings
from the
Andy Williams Collection

Ann Lane Hedlund

with a personal introduction by
Bill Pearson

THE SAINT LOUIS ART MUSEUM
October 26, 1997 - January 4, 1998

Dedicated to my parents,
Jim and Doris Hedlund,
St. Louis residents for 25 years,
and
In memory of
Joe Ben Wheat
(1916-1997)

Edited by Mary Ann Steiner

Designed by Jon Cournoyer

Production assistant Lauri Kramer

Printed by Valcour Printing, Inc.

Photography by David Ulmer

ISBN #0-89178-075-0
Library of Congress Catalog Card Number: 97-069559

cover:
Transitional blanket/rug, chief's variant
c.1890
Tapestry weave, interlocked
Andy Williams Collection

Contents

Director's Foreword

Since the Santa Fe Trail was established in 1821, midwesterners have been attracted to the Southwest. The St. Louis community in particular has found this region to be fascinating with respect to its landscape and the rich cultural traditions of Native American societies. The state of Missouri has played an active role in the political events of the Southwest, since General Kearny and the Missouri Volunteers marched into Santa Fe in 1846 and wrested the territory from Mexican authority. By the time that the tracks were laid for the Santa Fe Railway in 1881, St. Louisans had become regular visitors as well as settlers in the area. During that time, Navajo weavings were gaining wide recognition. Generally, non-Native Americans bought an occasional textile to decorate their homes, usually a wall or floor covering. Yet some were becoming serious collectors, recognizing the high quality of this Native American tradition.

How the Andy Williams collection of Navajo weavings has come to visit the Art Museum is linked to the development of what some call the music capital of the United States, namely, Branson, Missouri. The success of the Branson venture captured the attention of Mr. Williams who eventually built the Moon River Theater and settled in Branson. Years later Ben Thompson, a collector from St. Louis who saw the Williams show, was struck by the Navajo weavings on display in the beautiful theater lobby. He gave an usher his card for Mr. Williams's reference. Later, Thompson was invited back to see the entire collection with a friend and expert on Navajo textiles. Subsequently photos of these textiles were shared at a collectors' breakfast in St. Louis. We at the Museum were truly impressed by the images of the weavings.

In the Fall of 1996 John Nunley, our curator of the Arts of Africa, Oceania, and the Americas, Mr. Thompson, and I went to Branson, saw an absolutely wonderful show, and later were escorted to Mr. William's dressing room. We discussed the project and agreed to meet the singer the next morning to review the collection at his beautiful residence. We were all impressed by the quality of the chief's blankets, eye dazzlers, sarapes, and Moqui stripe blankets.

In discussions with John Nunley and Zoe Perkins, textile conservator at the Museum, we invited Ann Lane Hedlund to write the catalogue for the exhibition and to help us carry out the selection and presentation of the exhibition. Dr. Hedlund, Associate Professor at Arizona State University, Tempe, has organized numerous exhibitions, including *Contemporary Navajo Weaving: The Gloria F. Ross Collection of the Denver Art Museum* which has traveled to the Renwick Gallery, Smithsonian Institution, and the National Museum of the American Indian in New York as well as other institutions. Her intensive field work with American Indian weavers along with her knowledge and experience have been much appreciated in the preparation of the catalogue as well as the exhibition.

I would like to thank Ben Thompson, John Nunley and Zoe Annis Perkins for their efforts and enthusiasm in presenting this outstanding collection to our St. Louis community. I would also like to express my gratitude to Ann Hedlund whose very busy schedule did not dissuade her from this collaboration. A special acknowledgment to Leslie Claxton, Mr. Williams's personal assistant, for making arrangements for all parties to view and assemble the collection in Branson. Finally, a great praise song for Andy Williams who is a true collector of art and whose eye and generosity have made this exhibition possible; and to his long time friend Bill Pearson whose introduction to this text reveals yet another part of the story.

James D. Burke
Director

A Personal Introduction

I first met Andrew in an empty airplane hanger in Ketchum, Idaho, when Mr. Harriman and the railroad owned Sun Valley, and a bellhop named Paul secretly ran the world-famous ski resort. There was a blizzard raging outside while Andrew and his family and I tried to keep warm, waiting for our private planes to arrive. Mine was arranged by Paul and Andrew's by a friend of a friend.

When at last there came a break in the weather and both planes landed, one was a single engine Model T and the other a twin engine, chrome-plated beauty. Andrew and I knew our places in life, and I dutifully walked to the wreck, whereupon I was told it was Andrew's. Never have we laughed so hard, both pointing to the other's plane.

From that day thirty years ago, we have remained fast friends. Few today can count themselves so lucky. Of all the rich and famous that I have met throughout my life, no one has come close to Andrew's taste in art as well as life. No one has assembled such a catholic collection, from Diebenkorn to Baule bobbins. This collection is but one of several.

Andrew had been asked by the Queen of England to give some concerts at the Royal Albert Hall in London. He invited me to be his guest, so off we went. London then as now is an art collector's heaven—no race of people are as varied in their collecting. The French collect French; German, German; Italian, Italian; but the English collect everything.

Andrew's first discovery was a small shop on Pimlico Road selling jewel-like working steam engines built by ex-engineers and model makers. Unlike most models these actually worked, and again we laughed till tears came to our eyes as each of us with a tiny model shovel put miniature cardiff coal into a boiler and the engines began to run.

By the time Andrew had finished his concerts he had acquired over 20 of these beautiful working steam engines, including the famous "Gooch"—a model of the locomotive that held the record as the fastest train in the world. Today it is still in his bedroom on its special stand.

On this same trip, Andrew also acquired a dinner service of Chinese export porcelain with portraits of the rare animals of the world painted in 1710. Such is the consequence of his catholic collecting.

As we are both artaholics, I was invited to Japan where he was doing a singing tour. Of course Andrew again began collecting antiques. Only this time, it was exquisite hand-woven textiles of gold and silver thread that were used as wedding kimonos, intended to be worn only once. As we traveled Japan, Andrew bought more of them until he owned over 80 antique wedding kimonos. Now, twenty-five years later, he is using them in his new show in Branson, Missouri. I am sure the display will be breathtaking, as each is a masterpiece.

His collection of Native American textiles was formed over a period of ten years from 1975 to 1985. Originally this included many cultures—Saltillo, Rio Grande, Chimayo, and Pueblo—but because of some poor advice Andrew separated these variant cultures from his collection. The beneficiary of this decision was the De Young Museum. His current collection is but half of the original.

Once during the early stages of his Native American collecting I acquired a beautiful third phase chief's blanket for Andrew and suggested he hang it in his dining room, where he had just hung an important Rothko. It was done.

A month later, I found the blanket gone and asked Andrew why. Laughing he answered, "Billy I just paid $300,000 for that painting (it later sold for $1,700,000) and you hang a Navajo blanket on the other wall and no one looks at the Rothko." I had to laugh, too—there is great power in these wonderful weavings.

At this time Andrew was one of just a handful of people collecting these beautiful textiles. Dealers and Native Americans wrote him, offering some great family treasures. Andrew was so busy with his TV show that he had no time to actively pursue these offerings, so he asked me to go into the field and evaluate them.

On one such trip I went to see a group of seven Navajo weavings offered by a California dealer. Never had I seen such wonderful pieces, all classics and chief-style patterns. I advised Andrew to buy them, which he did. When I brought them to his Hollywood home and we spread them out to examine and admire them, one of them reminded Andrew of a blanket he had seen in the Harvey Collection that William Randolph Hearst had bought. I kept thinking about it for another week and then it came to me. Hearst had given that collection to a major museum many years ago.

I called the museum and asked if they were missing any Harvey-Hearst Navajo weavings. I was told that they would look into it. When I hadn't heard from them in another week I again called them but this time I talked with the director. A few days later I received an excited call from the director, saying that indeed some of their most important weavings were missing. I telephoned the dealer that we bought them from and got Andrew's money returned, and the museum once again had their blankets.

To this day Andrew and I still remember the beauty of those blankets and how wonderful they would have looked in his collection.

Such is my friend Andrew, who is as rare as the art he collects.

Bill Pearson

Tapestry in Motion
The Navajo Textile Tradition

Ann Lane Hedlund

During the mid-1600s, Navajo women borrowed the techniques of neighboring Pueblo Indian weavers and learned to make loomwoven fabrics.[1] Within several generations, Navajo weavers dramatically expanded the repertoire of traditional Pueblo design, using a newly adapted technique called tapestry weave and the addition of colorful trade yarns. To the somber palette and subtle patterning of the Pueblo fabrics, the Navajos added vibrant blocks of color and dynamic geometry. Through the use of tapestry weave, it became possible to create all the brilliant patterns of chief's blankets, eye dazzlers, and the varied textiles that followed.

The Andy Williams collection spans seven decades of Navajo weaving, from about 1850 to 1920. The fifty pieces included here represent the graphic power of late 19th-century Navajo weaving. Indeed, each textile was selected by Andy Williams for its visual strength and must hold its own within his larger collection of art from other times and places. Acquired between 1975 and 1985, these textiles have adorned Andy Williams's homes and offices and provide an important visual focus at his theater in Branson, Missouri.

This essay focuses upon the resilient character of Navajo weaving, specifically during the second half of the 19th century. The history of Navajo textiles prior to 1920 breaks roughly into three primary phases of development: (1) the classic/late classic period (1650-1875) of wearing blankets and other handwoven garments; (2) the transition period (1875-1895) that saw a move from blanket to rug weaving; and (3) the early rug period (1895-1920) in which weavers created custom-order rugs for the trade, among other things.[2] Throughout, weavers readily incorporated new elements while not losing sight of their Navajo identity, in essence continuously recreating themselves in the face of change.

One of the most intriguing aspects of the 19th-century blankets and rugs in the Williams collection is that the same designs—those taken from chief's blankets, women's blankets, and Moqui stripes—appear on textiles made for different uses, with differing materials, dyes, weights, and textures, during each of the three periods of Navajo textiles. The same design, for instance, appears on a refined classic blanket that was spun and woven so tightly that it is nearly waterproof and also on a rough transitional blanket with yarns so thick and loose that your fingers could poke through. The practice

Pictorial blanket/rug, c. 1880s; tapestry weave, interlocked, diagonal, and eccentric; 72 x 51 inches

continues today (Figure 1). Where did these designs come from and under what circumstances were they recycled? Did these designs persist through the generations or were they rediscovered and revived?[3]

In the next two sections, a discussion of Pueblo textiles presents the prototypes for Navajo weaving, and an explanation of tapestry weave describes the basic building block for Navajo textiles. Then, an overview of early Navajo history demonstrates the forces that influenced weaving over several centuries. Descriptions of the 19th-century Navajo textile tradition follow. The changes occurring during the last quarter of the century are outlined and their impact on weaving is described. The final section, prior to conclusions, addresses questions about who controlled rug designs at the turn of the century and explores the weavers' roles as inventors of their own tradition. The Andy Williams collection of classic and late classic blankets, transitional blankets and rugs, and custom-order revival rugs is illustrated, with notes on technique and construction. For readers who want further information, a selected bibliography concludes this volume.

FIGURE 1.
Navajo weavers today continue to draw upon 19th-century blanket patterns as inspiration for their rugs. Mary Lee Begay creates a contemporary "revival" style. Courtesy Ann Lane Hedlund, 1980.

Pueblo weaving

The Pueblo weaving tradition is comparatively conservative. Over the centuries, relatively few changes occurred in basic textile functions, forms, tools, and techniques, reflecting a strong continuity from prehistoric times through at least the early 20th century. The prehistoric repertoire was apparently more diverse than what survived into the late 1800s, but the more limited garment types prevalent in the 19th century almost all have considerably earlier antecedents. So far as we know, men were the primary weavers in most of the Pueblos, except at Zuni and perhaps several other villages. They wove within their homes and also inside religious structures known as kivas where various sacred rituals were regularly performed. The buildings' frameworks supported upright looms. For example, the one-piece woman's dress (see Nos. 1, 2), which would have been wrapped around the body, under one arm and over the other shoulder, has remained the same in format and essential qualities since at least the 14th century, when the same style was depicted on murals inside Pottery Mound kivas (Hibben 1975: Figures 45, 74, 99, 100). Men's kilts, sashes, and leggings also appear in the wall paintings, looking nearly as fresh as if taken from modern-day dance scenes. With the advent of Spanish wool and indigo, the raw materials and dyes changed, but the basic Puebloan forms and functions remained constant.

FIGURE 2.
Hopi man weaving on an upright loom supported from roof beams and anchored into the floor (in contrast to the more mobile Navajo looms lashed to trees or freestanding frames); note the slightly wider-than-long fabric on the loom. Photographed at Shungopavi, Second Mesa, Arizona. Courtesy Museum of Northern Arizona Photo Archives, MS168-3-20, J.W. Hildebrand collection, 1896.

Early Pueblo textiles were made from native cotton, apocynum (a linen-like native plant fiber), other vegetal fibers, and occasional animal fibers (dog, mountain goat, rabbit), colored by a variety of native dyes and pigments. Once the Spaniards brought goats and sheep into the Southwest, beginning in 1598, Pueblo weavers incorporated sheep's wool into their textiles. They also added blue indigo dye imported from Mexico. This blue, plus the natural fiber colors—white, gray, brown, black—represented the main color scheme for most textiles in the Pueblo repertoire. In the late 19th century, the same imported wool yarns that found their way into Navajo blankets—red yarns raveled from whole cloth (bayeta) and a series of multihued commercial yarns (Germantown and other brand names)—appear in Pueblo textiles, but used as subtle accents and only in small design areas. In contrast, Navajo weaving employs these same materials for dominant designs in unending variations.

Pueblo dresses, shawls, and some kilts are woven on the loom in a wider-than-long format (Figure 2). Most blankets, sashes, and loin cloths are the reverse, woven longer-than-wide. This distinction has implications for the size of the loom (that is, if wider-than-long fabrics are woven, they generally require a wider loom; longer fabrics mean some kind of vertical adjustment for the loom but smaller overall space requirements). Most Pueblo textile designs depend upon the regular repetition of geometric elements such as the small and subtle diamonds in a twill weave (Nos. 1, 2, detail of diamond twill). Patterns may also be composed of highly stylized motifs, as in ceremonial sashes, kilts, and manta borders, which rarely stray from a standard form and layout.

Pueblo weavers used a number of weaves. Balanced plain weave and balanced twill weave (diamond or herringbone patterns) are two of the most common, used in dresses, shawls, and other wrap garments. Ceremonial cotton or wool sashes were, and still are, patterned with a supplementary wool weft ("brocade") weave, and cotton kilts are usually embroidered by hand with commercial wool yarns on plain weave. Braiding is used for white cotton dance sashes; warp-faced float weaves are used for other belts. Most Pueblo blankets and rugs contain simple stripes in weft-faced plain weave; only occasionally are they created with tapestry weave when fancier designs are desired.

FIGURE 3.
Navajo tapestry weaving, in progress (detail), by Evelyn Curley of Ganado, Arizona. Courtesy Ann Lane Hedlund, 1983.

Tapestry weave

Tapestry weave can be described technically as "weft-faced plain weave with discontinuous weft patterning" (Emery 1966). But what does this mean? Plain weave is a fabric structure in which the weft yarns interlace over-one, under-one across the foundation warp yarns. Weavers worldwide use this technique in myriad variations. Weft-faced means that as the wefts interlace across the warps, they hide the warps from view. This results from having thicker wefts than warps and/or having the warps relatively more widely spaced. Alternatives to weft-faced are the warp-faced weave and balanced weave (in which both warp and weft are partially visible). Weft patterning occurs when the weft yarns change colors and dominate the designs. Other ways to create design include warp patterning (in warp-faced fabrics) and supplementary or complementary patterning in which additional yarns are added into the fabric. Discontinuous weft patterning indicates that, in order to make designs, the colored weft threads

a

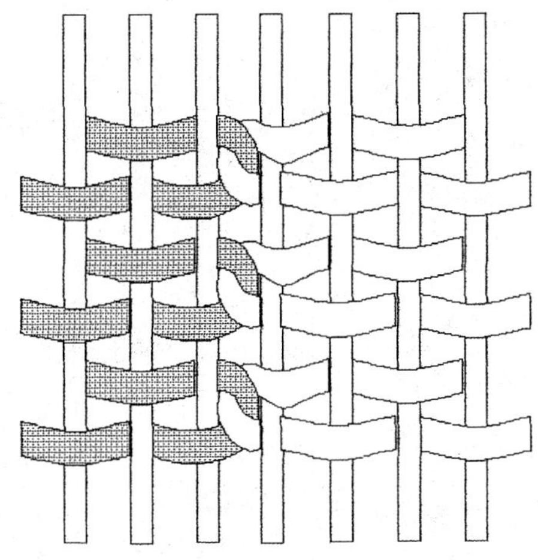

b

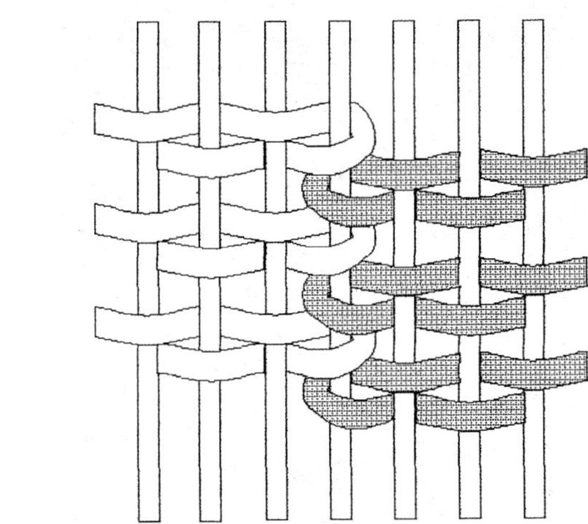

c

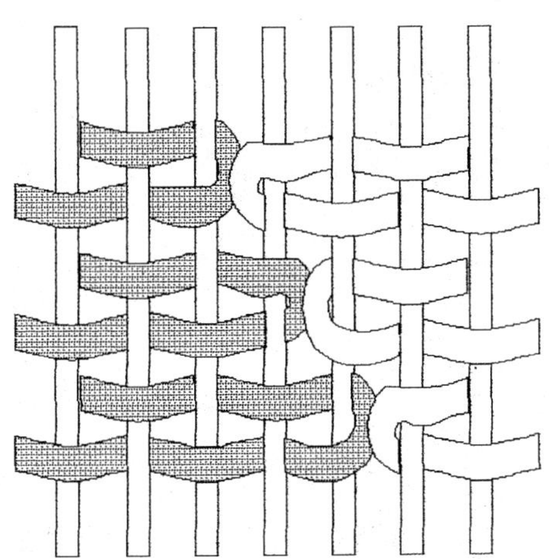

FIGURE 4.
Tapestry weave variations: a. Interlocked tapestry join; b. Dovetailed tapestry join; c. Diagonal tapestry join. Drawing courtesy Kit Schweitzer, 1997.

do not pass all the way across the fabric; they only weave certain segments before another color is introduced. Continuous weft patterning quite simply produces a series of horizontal bands across the fabric; discontinuous patterning, on the other hand, allows creation of almost any kind of design (Figure 3).

The southwestern-style loom is set up in an identical fashion for making either plain weave or tapestry weave. The tools are exactly the same for both—tapestry weave requires no more and no less equipment. The design areas in tapestry weave are picked out with the fingers, and the yarns to create them are woven in segments.

Where colors come together in a pattern, the weaver must decide how to join the colored areas. The simplest, but not strongest, way is to weave in short segments and leave a small slit between adjacent colors. To avoid creating a slit in the fabric, most weavers use either an interlocking join (see diagram 4a) or a dovetailed join (see diagram 4b). A diagonal join (see diagram 4c) requires no special manipulation of the yarns; in following a diagonal stairstep with two colors, all but the tiniest slits are avoided. A single textile may contain all these different joins or just one or two of them.

Tapestry weave may also be combined with twill weave instead of with plain weave. In the most common twill weave, weft yarns interlace over-two, under-two with the warps, creating a diagonal texture in the fabric. When tapestry technique is added, blocks of color appear on a diagonal (or diamond) textured surface. The well-known Kashmir shawls from southern Asia are made with twill tapestry weave. So are some Navajo saddle blankets of the late 19th century (see Nos. 22, 23, 24, 25).

Tapestry weave was used minimally by prehistoric southwestern weavers. The technique appears in narrow finger-woven bands that date to A.D. 400-700 and recurs occasionally in larger textiles of the 1300s.[4] The historic Pueblo repertoire of handwoven textiles includes blankets and sarapes, but most of these were made with weft-faced stripes in plain weave rather than tapestry weave. Occasionally Pueblo blankets contain tapestry patterning, but these were made during the late 19th and early 20th centuries, not early enough to link with the 17th and 18th-century period when Navajos acquired the basics from Pueblo weavers.

In fact, tapestry weave may have moved in the reverse direction, from Navajos to Pueblos. In two instances at Zuni at the turn of the 19th century, male weavers were reported as weaving "in the Navaho [sic] style" (Stevenson 1904:372-373, cited in Kent 1983b:49). There is further evidence from turn-of-the-century photographs that Pueblo weavers knew the tapestry technique, but these again are late and follow Navajo models.

Tapestry weave's capacity to create almost any kind of design makes the technique popular around the world—from ancient Inca tunics and painterly medieval wall coverings to delicate Chinese silk robes and modern Scandinavian carpets. Through generations of experimentation, the Navajos reinvented and perfected the technique for themselves.

Historical background

The Navajos originally arrived in the American Southwest sometime during the mid-14th century, from their homelands in the far north.[5] They are an Athabaskan-speaking people whose relatives include the Apache Indians of Arizona and New Mexico and, more distantly, the northern Athabaskans of Canada and Alaska. Spanish documents of the 16th and 17th centuries attest to the Navajos' semi-sedentary lifestyle with homes and fields established across present-day northern Arizona and New Mexico.[6] Groups of families formed localized bands, governed loosely by a local head man, rather than a chief who presided over everyone.

Navajo women are traditionally the principal landholders, property owners, and homemakers. Navajo families were, and to some extent still are, generally organized with a woman as head of household and with married children living close to the woman's family. Individuals trace their family line through their mother's ancestry (as opposed to the patrilineal descent that mainstream Euroamericans use, with their last names coming from their father's family). Women and men generally share in decision-making and leadership. Men play central roles in political and religious spheres and are often engaged in economic and civic activities beyond the family's boundaries.

According to longstanding cultural ideals, Navajo individuals have the power to make decisions and to act autonomously, from birth to final breath. Each person is responsible for his or her own actions. No one presumes to speak for an other. Verbal commands, even in child rearing, are rare. Instead, learning takes place by watching as a skill is demonstrated, not by direct instruction. A Navajo farmer, for example, would not imagine telling someone else where or when to plant; a weaver would never tell her neighbors how to make their rugs. Such individual freedom forms the basis of Navajo society and provides a framework for understanding the Navajos' history, their interactions with other peoples, and their cultural practices, whether herding sheep, designing a rug, or participating in a ceremony (Figure 5).

Relations with their newfound Pueblo neighbors brought significant changes to Navajo culture. Navajo men and women, who had been focused upon hunting and gathering before they migrated to the south, continued to pursue game animals and gather wild plant foods. But under Pueblo influence, they added farming and, with the introduction of Spanish livestock in the 1600s, herding and animal husbandry to their subsistence skills. Some aspects of Navajo religion today show evidence of Pueblo traits absorbed into a native

Navajo framework (Brugge 1983:491-495) And certainly one of the best-known contributions from Pueblo culture was the introduction of blanket weaving.

FIGURE 5.
Navajos have always lived independently in widespread settlements across their land. Their sheep represent self-sufficiency and life's essentials--living close to Mother Earth, feeding and clothing one's family, and reproducing with abundance. Courtesy Ann Lane Hedlund, 1994.

Relationships among neighboring groups were far from peaceful. Raiding for livestock and slaves and territorial warfare often occurred among the different peoples who came to settle in the Southwest: Pueblo, Navajo, Havasupai, Apache, Ute, Southern Paiute, Spanish and, later, Euroamericans. Records of the many altercations suggest that, although intermarriage, cultural exchanges, and annual trade fairs took place among the larger population, each ethnic group sought to express its own identity. Navajos rejected the Spanish missionary efforts and struggled to retain their seminomadic way of life. Pueblo people, on the other hand, at first suffered the Spanish who established missions in their villages. In 1680, however, the Pueblos united against the Spanish and temporarily drove them out of northern New Mexico. Fearing reprisal from the Spanish, many Pueblo individuals sought refuge with Navajo groups living to the west of the Rio Grande Valley. These refugees undoubtedly reinforced the weaving skills that Navajos had acquired some decades earlier. By the early 1700s Navajos were known to grow and weave cotton, to maintain sheep herds, and to weave wool blankets. They also traded their textiles and other goods extensively with other Indians and the Spanish (Wheat 1988).

The 19th century brought several landmark events to bear on Navajo lives. In 1821, Mexico gained possession of the Southwest from Spain but proved unable to control these hinterlands. Also in 1821, the Santa Fe Trail connected New Mexico with the central United States, opening up important trade opportunities. By 1846, the Southwest changed hands again and joined the Union. These newly acquired U.S. territories continued attracting new peoples—government agents, military personnel, American explorers, entrepreneurs, settlers, and Christian missionaries.

In 1863 the collision of peoples gained crisis proportions, and U.S. Army Colonel Kit Carson was sent to forcibly relocate the Navajos to Fort Sumner in eastern New Mexico. Members of the tribe persevered through the wrenching experiences of military domination and loss of their homes. People still talk of the disasters. Thousands died and the rest barely survived at Fort Sumner, also called Bosque Redondo, where the rations were meager, land was poor, and the culture was alien. Navajo people faced a barrage of change—different clothing, foods, behaviors, language. The survivors were released to return to Navajo country five years later, in 1868, only to discover their homes had been burned and their croplands destroyed. The resilient and resourceful Navajo character was further forged through such hard times—an independent and proud spirit persisted in each adversity. And despite the hardships, women's creativity expressed through blanket weaving remained alive, almost miraculously.

Navajo weaving—a tradition of invention

Navajo narratives tell how Spider Woman and Spider Man brought the first loom and weaving to the Navajo people in the earliest times. In keeping with the Navajos' values for individualism, these Holy People expected weavers to create new designs of their own with their newfound tools. Songs, prayers, and ritual activities all attest to the central nature of weaving in Navajo life for a very long time. Weaving continues to have a deep-seated significance to those who practice it. The gifts of Spider Woman and Spider Man provided weavers the means from which new traditions continue to spring (Figure 6).

By anthropologists' reckoning, some time around 1650 the Navajos adopted the Pueblo-style upright loom and moved it out of doors and into their homes (Wheat 1984:14). Their wooden hand tools—the spindles for making yarn, battens for dividing the yarns on the loom, and the combs which pack the yarn into place—reflect Pueblo prototypes. The earliest Navajo blankets contained native cotton rather than wool from the sheep introduced from Spain. The outward form of many

FIGURE 6.
Since early times when the Spider People brought weaving to the Navajos, looms have represented important spiritual elements. The first loom is said to have been made of sky and earth cords; sun rays and rock crystal; turquoise, abalone and white shell; and sheet, zigzag, and flash lightning (Reichard 1934). Courtesy Ann Lane Hedlund, 1981.

FIGURE 7.
Blankets were worn and used in a variety of ways by Navajo people. Here a mother and her two children are sheltered by their handwoven blankets. Courtesy of Museum of Northern Arizona Photo Archives, MS168-4-23, J.W. Hildebrand collection, 1896.

Navajo textiles as well as minute construction details resemble Pueblo fabrics—woven wider than long, with twined selvage cords and knotted corner tassels.

Both origin stories emphasize weaving as an activity introduced to the Navajos from the outside. Both also reflect the Navajos' ability to innovate and improvise as well as incorporate. Weaving rapidly became a useful part of Navajo culture and an integral part of its traditions. Indeed, Navajo culture revolves around the capacity to change and to create new possibilities for reinterpreting tradition.[7]

While the Navajos borrowed extensively from their original teachers, they modified the processes and products from the beginning. For instance, unlike most Pueblo textiles, Navajo ones usually contain "lazy lines" which are subtle diagonal lines across a solid colored area where the weaver has broken her field into several separate segments (usually done so that she need not reach across an entire fabric to interlace her yarn). Also, Navajo textiles are predominantly weft-faced rather than having a more balanced Pueblo-style weave (equal amounts of warp and weft visible in the weave). Navajos quickly replaced cotton with handspun sheep's wool, a more dyeable fiber. They eagerly sought commercially dyed yarns to add even more color to their blankets; among them were early 3-ply Saxony yarns and later 3- and 4-ply Germantown yarns (named for the Pennsylvania mill town where some of the yarns were manufactured). Navajo weavers also pioneered the technique of unraveling trade cloth (Spanish and Mexican bayeta and, later, American flannels) to obtain red yarns to reweave into their blankets. And beyond changing their blankets' texture and colors, they began creating elaborate designs through the use of tapestry weave.

While Navajo weavers did not necessarily originate the tapestry technique, the idea to use it extensively in their blankets, beginning by the early 1800s, seems to have been original. There is a notable relationship between tapestry weaving and the basket-making traditions of Navajo women (Kent 1985: 9). Indeed, their technique for making decorated coiled baskets requires the use of discontinuous elements in a tapestry-like fashion. Many of the classic Navajo blanket motifs—crosses, stepped diamonds and triangles, hooked elements—are also found on early Navajo baskets (Wheat 1984:16; 1995). Once the tapestry notion took hold, Navajo weavers expanded the weave's usefulness and exploited its design capacity like no others before them.

Navajo garment types, 1850-1880

Historic photographs and textiles from museum collections suggest that, among the Navajos, five major garment types were woven, worn, and traded by the third quarter of the 19th century: women's dresses; women's shawls; chiefs' blankets (and women's variations); banded blankets; and sarape-style blankets (Figure 7). All are represented in the Williams collection. In addition, smaller items such as sash belts, garters, hair ties, cradle bands, and saddle cinches were produced.

Women's two-piece dresses (No. 3) and shawls (No. 4) derive from Pueblo antecedents but have wide red borders with tapestry patterning at the top and bottom. How the one-piece, wider-than-long Pueblo dress which wrapped around the body became the Navajo two-piece, longer-than-wide model, which is worn somewhat like a sandwich board, remains a mystery. Perhaps the two-piece format grew out of the northern tradition of using two hides as the front and back of a dress. Whatever the inspiration, the innovation became firmly integrated into the standard Navajo repertoire of garments until replaced by purchased velveteen and calico cotton fabrics for tailored blouses and gathered skirts.

Chiefs' blankets got their name from the misconception that high-level Navajo chiefs wore them. The Navajo people were guided by local leaders, but did not have overall "chiefs" like some other tribes. Nevertheless, chiefs' blankets represent some of the finest of Navajo weaving, clearly prized by anyone fortunate enough to wear one. Woven wider-than-long, chief's-style blankets can be defined by four phases. The first phase is characterized by a series of horizontal bands in white and brown-black, with blue (and sometimes red) bands punctuating the blanket's end and middle zones (No. 6). The second phase adds three rectangular blocks of color, usually red with small geometric motifs, across each of the blanket's ends and middle; the alternating white and brown-black bands remain between the three colored zones (No. 7). In the third phase, the red blocks transform into diamonds or triangles, often with concentric layers of color; the white and black bands appear as background to the dominant red motifs which usually number nine or twelve (Nos. 8, 9). The fourth phase allows the diamonds and triangles to expand and dominate, nearly covering the background of white and black bands (No. 10). When worn around the shoulders, the patterns at each end of a chiefs' blanket connect to form a continuous design around the body.

Women's blankets represent a variation of the standard chief's styles. Designed in the same format, they are usually smaller in scale and have narrower banding in gray and black rather than white and black. While all four phases occur in women's blankets, the most common patterning is either second phase (No. 12) or a variant with a row of repeated motifs across each of the three design bands (No. 11).

The banded blankets closely resemble Pueblo antecedents. They are woven longer-than-wide, with varied rhythms of striping and color combinations. One common banded style is the so-called Moqui stripe, named with an alternate (and archaic) term for the Hopi Indians who wore striped blankets. This style uses zones of narrow blue and brown-black banding as its basis. These zones might alternate with plain white or other colored bands (Nos. 14 and 15). In later versions, weavers superimpose bold red triangles, diamonds, or other motifs onto the banded "background" (Nos. 16, 17) .

Sarape-style blankets are the most varied of the Navajo textile types. Many contain stepped elements borrowed from basketry and dress borders—terraced zigzags, triangles, diamonds, crosses, and other rectilinear motifs (Nos. 5, 18). Additional inspiration from Mexican sarapes, especially those from Saltillo, shows in their longer-than-wide format and the frequent use of serrated zigzags and diamonds along with many jagged filler motifs (Figure 8). Layouts of the sarapes range from all-over patterning to central or radiating designs to a series of horizontal banded zones. The type includes unusual treatments such as the wedge weave. Ponchos, another form of sarape, have woven-in neckholes. Sarapes come in small sizes for children and bigger sizes that could fit a pregnant woman or a large man.

The transitional period

The original boundaries of the Navajo Reservation were established by treaty in 1868, forever changing the long-held freedoms so valued by Navajo people. After their return from Bosque Redondo, families settled in widespread, loosely aggregated communities across northern New Mexico and Arizona and southern Utah. For ten years they received annuity distributions of household supplies including yarns, cloth, and clothing from the U.S. government. Military posts such as Fort Defiance and Fort Wingate served as suppliers of such commercial goods and eventually became the site of boarding schools and health clinics. Churches and missionaries established themselves. The railroad reached the southern border of the reservation in 1881, bringing jobs and more goods, as well as access to new markets. A growing number of trading posts stocked groceries and dry goods, exchanging them for Navajo sheep's wool and pelts, pinon nuts, other produce, and craftwork such as jewelry, baskets, and textiles. Mill-woven blankets and commercial cotton cloth began replacing handwoven blankets and garments. An economy based upon local barter slowly began to shift toward cash exchange and wage labor.

The period of 1890-1900 was marked by poor economic conditions, but simultaneously a boom time for weaving, ". . . when aniline dyes were a novelty and commercial demand an intoxicating stimulus" (Amsden 1934:189). David Brugge describes the situation: "The Panic of 1893 initiated a national depression that coincided with losses due to storms and drought in Navajo country. The hardships persisted until the turn of the century, and many trading posts went out of business. Craft work, especially weaving, increased dramatically as families tried to maximize the value of what they had to sell" (Brugge 1993:40).

FIGURE 8.
Navajo weaver working outdoors. Courtesy of Museum of Northern Arizona Photo Archives, MS168-4-44, J.W. Hildebrand collection, 1895-1908.

That period marks a transition in all aspects of Navajo life—social and material, political and personal. In some cases Navajo people embraced change and sought to incorporate it into their lives. Storebought goods, tools, and equipment were quickly integrated into Navajo households. Other changes, like those affecting family structure, sheep ownership, or widespread housing patterns, were met with clear resistance. Traditional Navajo values for family, livestock, and land persisted while people incorporated many relatively superficial, if highly visible, elements into their lifestyles.[8]

Transitional weaving

The transitional period signals major changes in Navajo weaving. The very look and feel of the textiles changed as blanket-weaving gave way to rug-making. Earlier garments and blankets, once created for domestic use and tribal trade, were replaced by handwoven floor rugs sold to an outside market.

Not only did Navajo weavers seem to have the general disposition to embrace change, but they had a dynamic and flexible tool—tapestry weave—to wield in the process.

The Navajos' internment at Bosque Redondo introduced weavers to new materials, such as colorful Germantown yarns, and to new design ideas like the elaborate serrate diamonds from Mexican sarapes. After their return from Bosque Redondo, commercial yarns along with other rations were issued to Navajo weavers by the U.S. government. Navajos adapted these into eye-dazzling designs of their own, exchanging their earlier horizontal bands for elaborate diamonds with a vertical orientation (Nos. 19, 20). By the late 1880s, ready access to aniline (synthetic) package dyes through local trading posts expanded the brilliant colors applied to native handspun wool (Nos. 39, 49).

Throughout Navajo country, trading posts established new approaches to weaving, first by offering mill-woven blankets and commercial cotton clothing as alternatives to handwoven garments, and secondly by encouraging the production of heavier textiles for trade. Often paid for by the pound at local trading posts, and hence the nickname "pound blankets," the resulting handwoven textiles were neither blankets nor rugs; rather they possessed an evolving mix of qualities. Most common were the soft, thickly spun wool blanket/rugs, called *diyogi* by Navajos (No. 38).

Generally speaking, pound blankets and rugs represent a decline in weaving quality. Paid by the pound, some weavers lost their incentive to excel and experiment. They left dirt and sand in their wool, which then weighed in at a higher price. An expedient but cheapening material, cotton string was first sold by the posts and later criticized by the same traders; it appears as warp in many pound blankets. Packaged aniline dyes, while producing bright colors, could also disfigure a rug: either their colors bled onto adjacent areas when washed, or they faded until a pattern disappeared.

To counter this decline, several traders provided models for "ideal" rug designs and urged tighter quality control. J. L. Hubbell of Ganado, Arizona, established an empire of trading posts beginning in the late 1870s and continuing until his death in 1930. C.N. Cotton, active from the 1880s until 1934 and based in Gallup, New Mexico, formed a partnership with Hubbell. They developed a wide market for Navajo crafts, and Cotton may have been the first to conceive of Navajo blankets as floor rugs (Williams 1989:33). Through their close business relationship with Hubbell, the Fred Harvey Company's buyers, J.F. Huckel and Herman Schweizer, expressed strong preferences for certain rug styles, colors, and materials (Howard and Pardue 1996:40-47). J. B. Moore traded at Crystal, New Mexico, only from 1897 to 1912, but had a significant impact on weavers. Responsive to an expanding American market for Indian-made goods, these traders encouraged certain designs, colors, and materials, and published mail order catalogues that reinforced certain images. They supplied wool, yarn, and dyes and discouraged the use of cotton string for warp. At the turn of the century, Hubbell offered 1-ply and 4-ply carpet yarns of a heavier weight, suitable for the larger floor rugs he advocated. Moore had wool cleaned and dyed under the supervision of his wife and a commercial mill before weavers wove it into their rugs.

In contrast to Moore's preferences for Oriental motifs and only occasional references to the classic blanket styles, J. L. Hubbell was completely taken with the older designs. He wrote, "I have been at the greatest pains to perpetuate the old patterns, colors, and weaves, now so rapidly passing out of existence even in the memory of the best weavers . . . I can supply genuine reproductions of the old weaves" (Hubbell cited in Blomberg 1988:6). He invited several artists to make small paintings depicting these older designs, mixed with occasional innovations, presumably to make them more marketable. To reinforce these designs in local weavers' minds, he displayed them prominently in the trading post at Ganado (as they are still displayed today). Of the ten designs included in Hubbell's 1902 mail order catalogue, six were patterned after "old style" blankets. Women's dresses (No. 28), shawls (Nos. 26, 27), women's blankets (Nos. 34, 35, 37), chief's blankets (No. 29), and Moqui striped designs (Nos. 30, 31, 32) became the core repertoire used in Hubbell revival rugs. Crosses were one of the most popular motifs (and indeed they appear in all of the Williams collection pieces just listed). Local weavers used tightly respun Germantown yarns and sturdy carpet yarns to recreate these images in a precise and regular fashion.[9]

FIGURE 9.
Sadie Curtis collects museum catalogues for their pictures of 19th-century blankets. Her chief blanket-rug on the loom is a composite of several different historic blankets plus her own imagination and was commissioned by a private collector. Courtesy Ann Lane Hedlund, 1981.

Simultaneously, other weavers recycled these very same images into loose handspun blankets, combining the qualities of pound blankets with imagery from classic/late classic weaving. Their work includes relatively close versions of earlier blankets (Nos. 34, 35, 36, 44) and more fanciful variations (No. 37), but never strictly imitates the earlier prototypes. Whether, and in what ways, these weavers were linked with Hubbell Trading Post is not known. Many of these contain cotton string warps rather than handspun wool warps. While traders Cotton, Hubbell, and Moore all claimed not to buy rugs with cotton warps, at various times they also admitted to doing so, even though paying "less for same and sell[ing] it cheaper" (Hubbell 1902, cited in Bauer 1987:53).

Weavers of the transition period also produced an interesting array of saddle blankets and pieces sold as small rugs. Single saddle blankets usually measure roughly 30 inches square; double saddle blankets, meant to be folded in half, are about 30 by 60. The weavers favored twill weave to create saddle blankets, maybe because it is stronger and thicker, but also perhaps because of the rich diagonal and diamond patterning that could be created (Nos. 22, 23, 24, 25). These blankets continued in native use long after handwoven garments became obsolete and at the same time became a popular buyer's item for ranch and home use.

By 1915 requests for the "old style" rugs with blanket designs had died out (Bauer 1987:91). The buying public sought floor rugs in natural colors with surrounding borders, and traders encouraged weavers to make these (No. 32). By 1921 Germantown blankets were almost entirely replaced, as J.L. Hubbell wrote, by "real native wool blankets, being an original indian art, and being more servicible [sic] than the other" (Bauer 1987:94).

Additionally, the Williams collection includes three textiles that reflect another design movement which developed during the transitional and early rug periods—the delightful trend of weaving pictorial images into blankets and rugs. Certainly tapestry weave was a perfect technique to employ in this way. The earliest pictorial motifs were single figures or rows of figures, usually animals, birds, or people, worked into the standard format of a striped blanket (No. 40). Gradually, pictorial elements took over the design space until they formed the main focus. Vehicles—trucks, trains, and planes—became a source of fascination (No. 41). Occasionally a weaver would abstract a design element from a larger image and repeat it to form a brand new design. Lettering from commercial packaging (flour sacks and coffee cans, for instance) and the stepped terraces of a traditional wedding basket (No. 50) offered new opportunities for innovation.

The reinvention of tradition

The appearance of designs from chief's blankets, women's blankets, and Moqui stripe blankets repeated in three different phases of Navajo weaving history raises questions about the respective roles of weavers and traders in designing rugs at the end of the 19th century. Did these designs persist through generations of Navajo families, or were they rediscovered and revived by enthusiastic entrepreneurs? Just who was responsible for the recycling of older designs?

Written records stress the traders' involvement; unfortunately, there is little to document the weavers' views.[10] Early discussions emphasize the traders' paternal and creative role in rugweaving from the 1880s on. Recent opinion has criticized the traders, specifically J. L. Hubbell, for an exploitive and domineering approach to Navajo weaving.[11] Undoubtedly the varied attitudes and behaviors practiced by different traders and different weavers could cover a wide spectrum, from subtle suggestions to firm demands and from passive acceptance to active rejection. The following discussion focuses on the weavers' roles and their ultimate control over design.

At the outset, we might ask why the older designs did appeal to the buyers, the traders, and the weavers. The buying public, above all, wanted "authenticity," a genuine Indian article. What better choice than something that looks old? Traders wanted to please the public and thereby earn a living. Weavers not only tried to please the traders in order to earn their living, but expressed their continuing values for family, land, and livestock by selecting designs that evoked earlier times. Each group was actively engaged in the construction of what they perceived to be Navajo "tradition."[12]

The Navajos' approach to design, from the very beginning, was "aggressive" (Berlant and Kahlenberg 1977:65). The earliest garment designs were instigated by Navajo weavers, without aid from traders or non-Indian buyers, by freely borrowing from many sources and responding to domestic and wider markets. This penchant for eclectic source materials presages weavers who later worked with traders and responded actively to their ideas and suggestions, without need for coercion. Weavers have rarely appeared to be passive recipients of suggested designs; they have come from a tradition that valued invention.

It is likely, but rarely acknowledged, that some Navajo weavers lived through the late 19th century and participated in several phases of weaving.[13] Despite short life expectancies, an individual might easily have woven bayeta dresses as a teenager, produced pound blankets as a 30 year old, and worked on Hubbell revival pieces by the time she was 50 at the turn of the century! Moreover, she might have continued to use similar designs even as her materials, purposes, and buyers were changing. There is no question that traders of her day encouraged certain designs over others, but the traders' suggestions, after all, were derived from earlier designs that she herself was using. Hubbell himself collected older Navajo blankets as models for the paintings which served as models for rugs.

FIGURE 10.
Hubbell Trading Post, now operated by the National Park Service, continues the tradition of encouraging weavers to adapt 19th-century designs for their modern rugs. Evelyn Curley, creating her version of a "Moqui stripe" pattern here, works for the post as a weaving demonstrator. Courtesy Ann Lane Hedlund, 1988.

By the late 19th century, weavers' work was clearly in a state that "remembers our great-great-great grandmothers that we've never seen," as one weaver living today reminds us. Their tools and processes represented continuity with the past while their lives moved into a new era. Their choice of blanket designs expressed ties to the past while the rug format proclaimed modernity. Altogether weaving reinforced Navajo culture with an emphasis on flexibility and individuality as part of the tradition.

Even when traders asked for specific designs, some weavers kept the traders guessing. One of C. N. Cotton's catalogues proclaims repeatedly, "NO DESIGN OF BLANKET IN THIS BOOK CAN BE REPRODUCED" (Williams 1989:74, 76, 78, 80, 82). Moore's 1911 catalogue describes his ideal approach:

"If the weaver is known to be strong on originating handsome designs, she is left to work out the pattern in her own way. But not all good weavers are good designers; so, for those who are not, we furnish patterns from our cuts, or from other rugs in stock for them to work to. Invariably, each will add some touch of individuality to her work and there is never any danger of monotony, no matter how many we may have weaving out designs that others have originated. There is always some difference between any two rugs" (Moore 1911:4; reproduced in Ricks and Anthony 1986).

Historian Ernie Bulow observes: "Traders in many parts of the growing reservation encouraged certain styles and color schemes, but Navajo weavers, coming out of a tradition of personal isolation and strong individuality, would always alter the patterns in some details . . . . At most, Moore's design influence was probably limited to suggestion and persuasion, along with the economic pressure he could bring to bear " (Bulow in Ricks and Anthony 1986:v).

Relationships are further unraveled if we compare Hubbell's approach to "his" Navajo weavers and the ways in which he and his male business associates communicated with each other. We should not presume that the same blunt style that passed between him, Cotton, Huckel, and Schweizer was also used with the weavers.[14] Instead, Hubbell hung paintings in his post to communicate with weavers. Although he spoke Navajo to some degree, he apparently chose also to use the Navajo way of showing, not telling, to influence weavers' decisions. He knew weavers were capable of remembering and replicating details after observing the paintings. Through direct experience he understood that outright demands would only result in resistance; suggestions led to cooperation (Brugge 1993).

Although Cotton, among others, flatly states, "No two Navajo Blankets are ever exactly alike, either in design or weave" (Williams 1989:75), the weavers defy such generalizations. Navajo weavers did occasionally repeat themselves and borrow directly from each other. Popular styles were duplicated or used as the basis for improvisation. And even with all their warnings, the traders themselves also claim, ". . . while we cannot always get exact sizes and designs, we can come near enough to satisfy the most fastidious" (Williams 1989:75). On the whole, weavers were neither so compliant as to compromise themselves entirely nor so resistant as to lose good business. Instead, they acted in a pragmatic and individual manner.

Concluding Remarks

In the blankets of the classic and late classic period, the earliest innovations came from a variety of sources: from Navajo basketry and Pueblo weaving, and from Spanish and Mexican materials and models. The Navajos developed tapestry weave to create wearing blankets of tremendous beauty and utility. The technical and trade revolutions of the late 19th century allowed Navajo weaving to flourish, with the creation of new designs and the recycling of older ones. In the later Hubbell revival rugs and the chief-style pound blankets, we witness both a continuity and a reinvention of tradition: chief's blankets, women's dresses, mantas, and Moqui stripes reappear in different fabrics and nostalgically remind observers and weavers alike of earlier times. The Navajos' serious economic needs resulted in their willingness to respond to traders' suggestions, but the response was always tempered by individual will. The Navajo weaver's ability to balance between continuity and innovation, choosing neither one exclusively, provided a way to deal with the barrage of new ideas and materials.

Weaving is a series of steps that combine conscious and unconscious decision-making; the woven products represent a set of choices and negotiations. Navajo weavers manipulate their weaving for both internal satisfaction and outward market gratification, and the two need not be in competition. Ultimately, Navajo weaving can be viewed as the result of complex interactions in which weavers, traders, and buyers come together to influence, depend upon, and test each other. An unusual adaptation of a chief's blanket in a "bull's eye" form (No. 13 and cover) illustrates the creative way in which one resilient Navajo weaver negotiated this terrain. In fact, each textile in the Andy Williams collection represents a weaver's unique and imaginative response to her circumstances.

Endnotes

1. Joe Ben Wheat has established that Navajos had acquired sheep by 1640 and that they must have been weaving by the middle of the 17th century, some time before the Pueblo revolt of 1680 (Wheat 1984:14).

2. Scholars vary somewhat on the dates for Navajo textile history, but most agree with the general trajectory of changes. Kent's (1985) time frame is comprised of the Classic period, 1650-1865; the Transition period, 1865-1895; and the Rug period, since 1895. Blomberg (1988) defines the Classic period from 1650 to 1868; the Transitional from 1868 to 1890; and the Rug period from 1890 to 1920. Rodee (1981) calls the latter the Transition Period, also dating it 1890-1920. I follow more closely the periods as defined by Joe Ben Wheat who includes a Late Classic period following the Classic. For recent developments, a regional rug period, 1920-1976, and a contemporary art period, since the mid-1970s, should be added.

3. While this essay focuses on the occurrence of these designs before 1920, in another article I reflect on the revival of these same styles after 1960 (Hedlund 1996). Indeed, the use of older designs never completely disappears at any time. Webster (1996) examines "three major movements of Navajo revival weaving" (p. 415): from 1890 to 1920, from 1920 to 1950, and after the 1950s. Acknowledging Navajo weavers' self-determination, she associates the earliest period with reservation traders' attempts to improve weaving quality; the second with growing art patronage and outsiders' efforts to preserve native culture; and the third with "formalized partnerships between prominent Navajo weavers and specific traders or retailers" (p. 416).

4. Kent notes that these were unusual and do not appear to continue into the historic weaving tradition of the Pueblo Indians. She also observes: "Plain weave tapestry was extremely rare as a technique for [loom] weaving cotton cloth, the only examples coming from Hidden House, a Sinagua site in the Verde Valley [ca. 1300 A.D.]. This seems odd since it is a simple way of building complex patterns that has been exploited to some degree by modern Pueblo weavers and extensively by Navajo weavers in making blankets and rugs. It is the same process that was used by the Basketmaker weavers in creating nonloom tumplines, cradle bands, and women's aprons, and it continued to be employed by Puebloans for these narrow articles through P III [Pueblo III period, A.D. 1100-1300]" (Kent 1983a:198).

5. Neither archaeologists nor Native Americans agree on exactly when Navajos arrived and settled in the Southwest, but archaeological data increasingly points to sometime in the 14th century (Brugge 1983:489-490).

6. Accounts of the Antonio de Espejo expedition of 1582-83 (Perez de Luxan 1929:86, 111-114) and the Benavides memorials of 1630 (1954), and 1634 (1945) are especially informative (cited in Brugge 1983:491).

7. John Farella emphasizes this when he writes that, for the Navajo people, " . . . to be traditional is to believe in change" (1984:195).

8. In his classic study of culture change, Evon Vogt identified the major means by which Navajos cope with change as an "incorporative" approach, as opposed to other models of "fusion" or "compartmentalization" (1961:328-329). Farella expands upon Vogt's views when he observes, "Externally, then, the Navajos have appeared to become more like Anglos, but I believe that this external change has been made in order to remain traditional. That is, I am proposing that in order for the Navajos to remain 'traditional' they have come to appear more and more Western" (1984:195).

9. Marian Rodee notes that most Hubbell revival blankets are "in pristine condition, almost as if the purchasers had acquired them as collectors items in the realization that the Classic period weaving was already rare and expensive" (1981:66).

10. Elsewhere I have discussed the difficulties of assessing native women's points of view from the historical record (Hedlund 1996:48-49). In that same essay, I also discuss Navajo weavers' current views of the older blanket tradition and how they incorporate ideas from it into their weaving today.

11. For a hypercritical reading of Hubbell's record, see M'Closkey (1994); for more supportive and balanced views, see Brugge (1993) and Blue (1986).

12. The construction, or reinvention, of traditions has become a focal topic for a number of scholars (see Anderson 1991; Hobsbawm and Ranger 1983).

13. Berlant and Kahlenberg (1977:61) note, "A Navajo weaver who was fifty years old in 1895 would have been nineteen at the time of the Navajo exile to Bosque Redondo. She would have lived through most of the major changes of style and technique affecting the Navajo blanket tradition."

14. Examples of correspondence between these men, excerpted from the Hubbell Papers (Special Collections, University of Arizona, Tucson), are cited in Howard and Pardue (1996), Blomberg (1988), and Bauer (1987).

Pueblo/Navajo Dresses and Child's Blanket

1

Pueblo woman's dress, c. 1870s

Balanced diamond and diagonal twill weaves
40 x 42 inches; 26 warps/inch, 28 wefts/inch

2

Pueblo woman's dress, c. 1900

Balanced diamond and diagonal twill weaves, embroidered
38 x 51 inches (unfolded); 20 warps/inch, 24 wefts/inch

3

Woman's two-piece dress, c. 1860-75

Tapestry weave, interlocked

51 1/2 x 35 inches each; 16 warps/inch, 80 wefts/inch

4

Woman's shawl, c. 1875

Weft-faced diagonal twill weave
41 x 52 inches; 12 warps/inch, 42 wefts/inch

5

Child's wearing blanket, c. 1850-60

Tapestry weave, interlocked
46 x 29 inches; 9 warps/inch, 52 wefts/inch

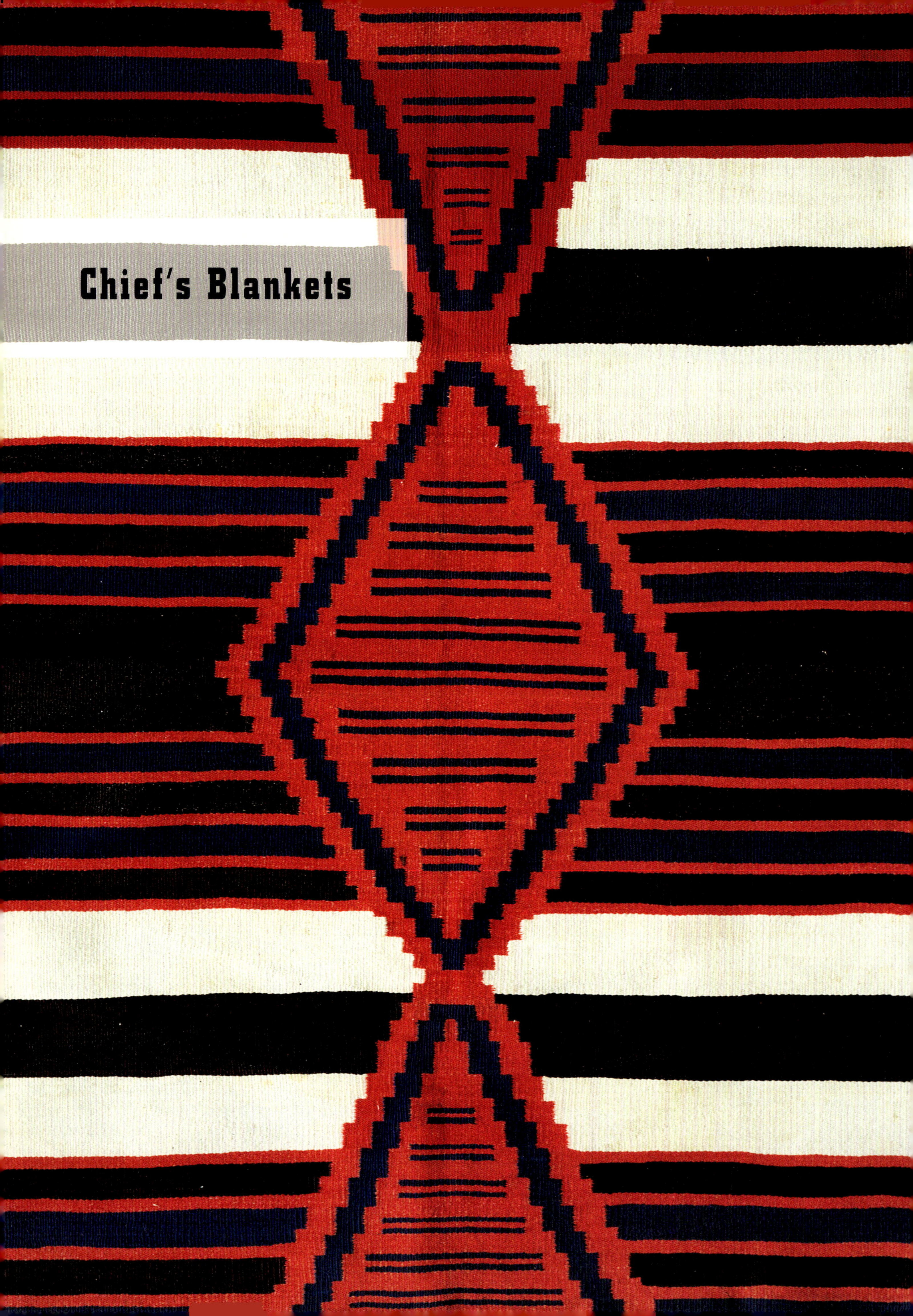

Chief's Blankets

6

Chief's blanket, c. 1870

Weft-faced plain weave
53 x 67 inches; 7 warps/inch, 26-40 wefts/inch

7

Chief's blanket, c. 1870s

Tapestry weave, dovetailed
53 x 67 inches; 7 warps/inch, 40-50 wefts/inch

8

Chief's blanket, c. 1870s

Tapestry weave, interlocked
56 x 75 inches; 9 warps/inch, 40 wefts/inch

9

Chief's blanket, c. 1870s

Tapestry weave, interlocked

54 x 69 inches; 8 warps/inch, 48 wefts/inch

10

Chief's blanket, c. 1870s

Tapestry weave, interlocked
54 x 78 inches; 8 warps/inch, 40-50 wefts/inch

11

Woman's blanket, c. 1880s

Tapestry weave, interlocked
42 x 50 inches; 8 warps/inch, 36 wefts/inch

12

Woman's blanket, c. 1880-85

Tapestry weave, interlocked
44 x 65 inches; 10 warps/inch, 40-46 wefts/inch

13

Transitional Chief's Blanket/Rug, c. 1890

Tapestry weave, interlocked
61 x 72 inches; 6 warps/inch, 38 wefts/inch

Moqui Stripe
Wearing Blankets

14

Wearing blanket, c. 1860-70s

Weft-faced plain weave

77 x 54 inches; 8 warps/inch, 30 wefts/inch

15

Wearing blanket, c. 1880

Weft-faced plain weave

71 x 53 inches; 9 warps/inch, 60 wefts/inch

16

Wearing blanket, c. 1880

Tapestry weave, interlocked
74 x 50 inches; 11 warps/inch, 56 wefts/inch

17

Wearing blanket, c. 1870s

Tapestry weave, diagonal
78 x 50 inches; 8 warps/inch, 30 wefts/inch

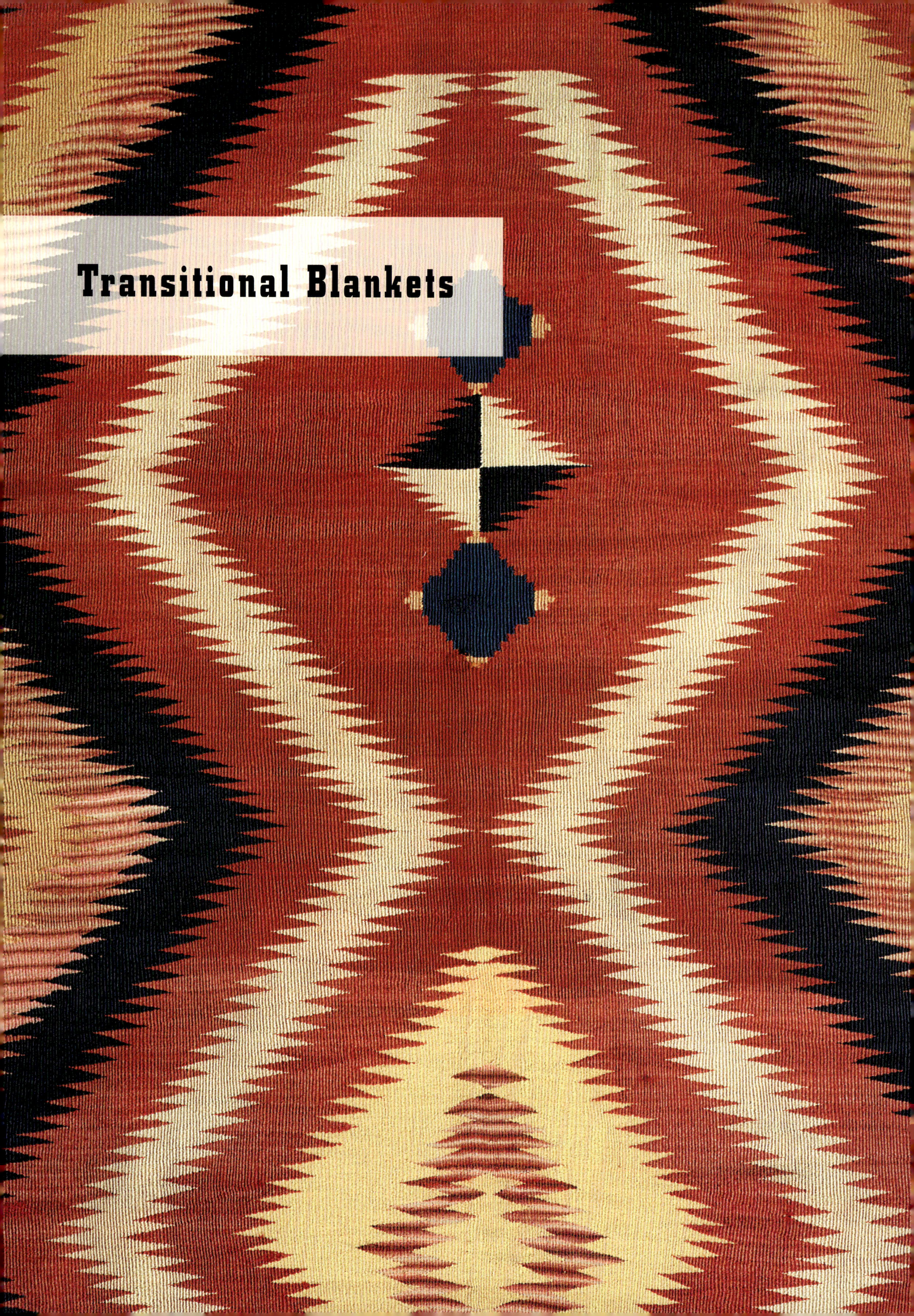

Transitional Blankets

18

Wearing blanket, c. 1880s

Tapestry weave, dovetailed
74 x 52 inches; 11 warps/inch, 44 wefts/inch

19

Transitional blanket, c. 1870

Tapestry weave, dovetailed and diagonal
75 x 50 inches; 9 warps/inch, 53 wefts/inch

20

Transitional blanket, c. 1880

Tapestry weave, interlocked and diagonal
82 x 60 inches; 10 warps/inch, 56 wefts/inch

Saddle Blankets/Small Rugs

21

Transitional rug/double saddle blanket, c. 1885

Tapestry weave, interlocked
52 x 33 inches; 11 warps/inch, 50 wefts/inch

22

Double saddle blanket, c. 1880s

Twill tapestry weave, interlocked and diagonal
48 x 31 inches; 9 warps/inch, 30 wefts/inch

23

Double saddle blanket/small rug, c. 1880s

Twill tapestry weave, interlocked
57 x 33 inches; 7 warps/inch, 28 wefts/inch

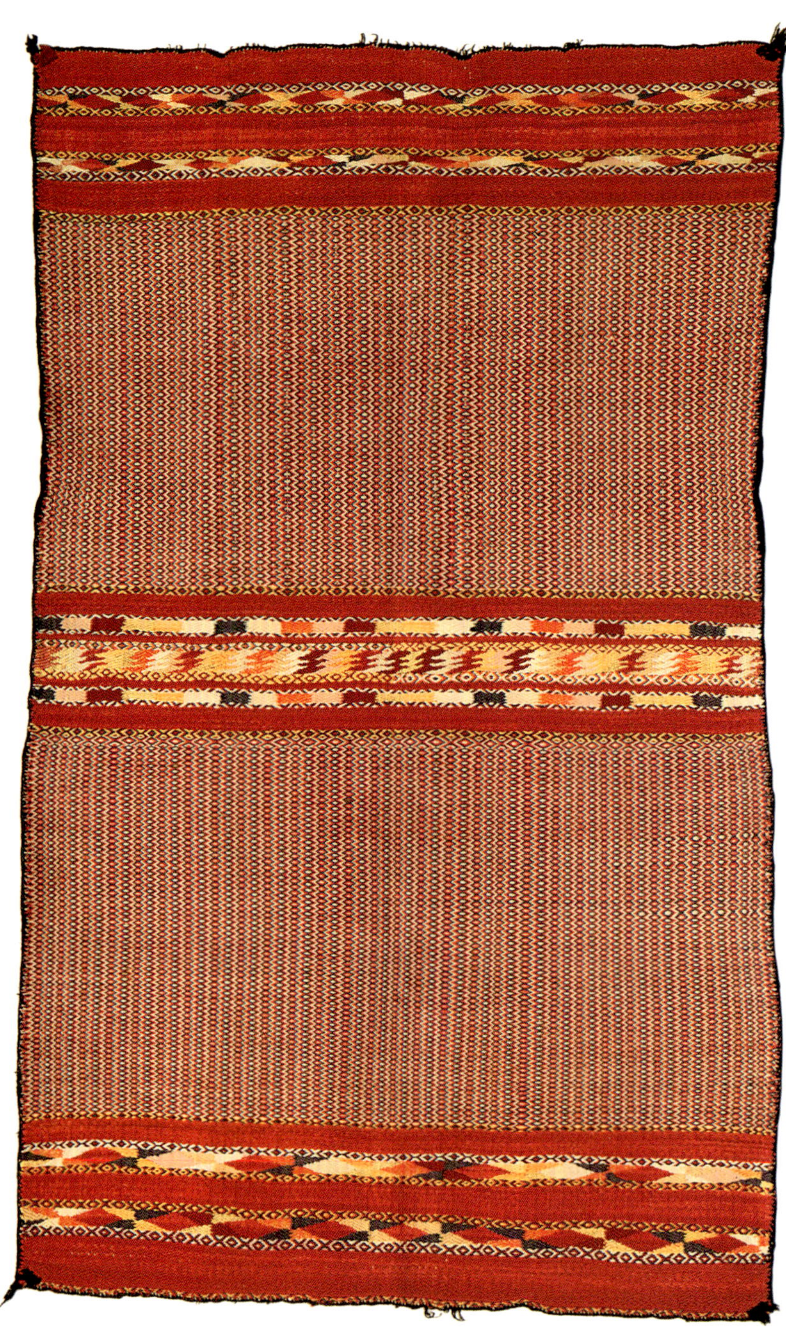

24

Double saddle blanket, c. 1880s

Diamond twill weave and twill tapestry weave, interlocked and diagonal
49 x 30 inches; 16 warps/inch, 48-60 wefts/inch

25

Double saddle blanket/small rug, c. 1880s

Twill tapestry weave, diagonal
53 x 31 inches; 11 warps/inch, 40 wefts/inch

Hubbell Revival Style

26

Transitional blanket/rug, c. 1890s

Woman's shawl pattern

Twill tapestry weave, dovetailed

47 x 64 inches; 11 warps/inch, 52 wefts/inch

27

Transitional blanket/rug, c. 1890s

Woman's shawl pattern
Tapestry weave, dovetailed
56 x 66 inches; 9 warps/inch, 40 wefts/inch

28

Transitional blanket/rug, c. 1890s

Woman's dress pattern

Tapestry weave, interlocked

51 x 31 inches; 10 warps/inch, 48 wefts/inch

29

Transitional blanket/rug, c.1890s

Chief's blanket pattern, 3rd phase variant
Tapestry weave, interlocked
66 x 52 inches; 10 warps/inch, 50 wefts/inch

30

Transitional blanket/rug, c. 1900

Moqui stripe pattern
Tapestry weave, dovetailed
51 x 57 inches; 8 warps/inch, 32 wefts/inch

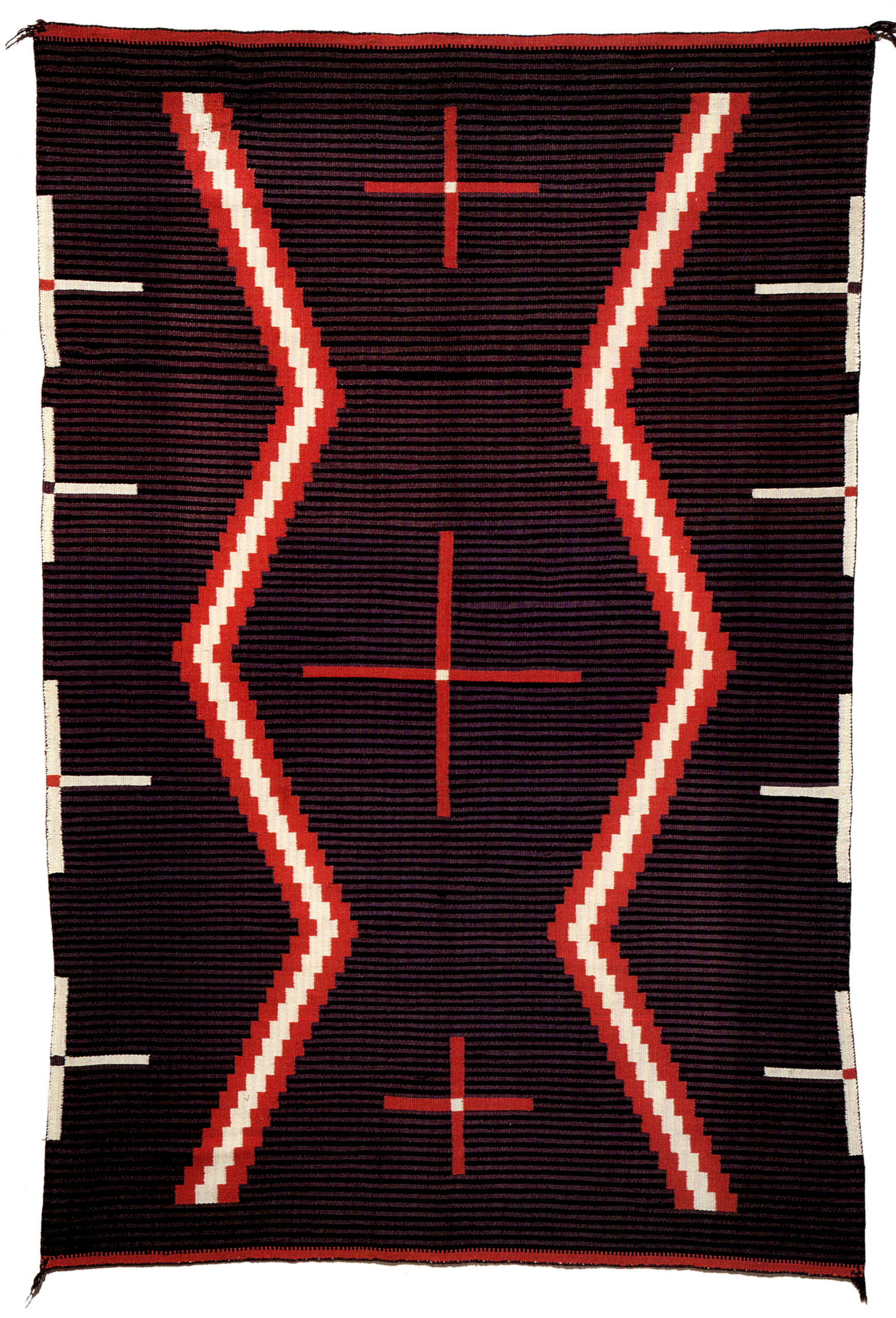

31

Transitional blanket/rug, c. 1890s

Moqui stripe pattern
Tapestry weave, interlocked
70 x 53 inches; 8 warps/inch, 36 wefts/inch

32

Transitional blanket/rug, c. 1890s

Moqui stripe pattern
Tapestry weave, dovetailed
77 x 62 inches; 8 warps/inch, 32 wefts/inch

33

Transitional rug, c. 1900-10

Tapestry weave, dovetailed

86 1/2 x 51 1/2 inches; 9 warps/inch, 42 wefts/inch

Pound Blankets

34

Transitional blanket, c. 1890s

Woman's chief-style pattern
Tapestry weave, diagonal
55 x 68 inches; 6 warps/inch, 18 wefts/inch

35

Pound blanket, c. 1880s

Woman's chief-style pattern
Tapestry weave, interlocked
50 x 67 inches; 7 warps/inch, 40 wefts/inch

36

Pound blanket, c. 1900

Woman's or chief's blanket pattern
Tapestry weave, interlocked
57 x 59 1/2 inches; 6 warps/inch, 18-26 wefts/inch

37

Pound blanket, c. 1890s

Woman's chief-style variant
Tapestry weave, dovetailed
36 1/2 x 53 inches; 5 warps/inch, 12 wefts/inch

38

Pound blanket, c. 1880s

Tapestry weave, diagonal
85 x 64 inches; 5 warps/inch, 16 wefts/inch

39

Pound blanket, c. 1880s

Tapestry weave, dovetailed and diagonal
72 x 53 inches; 7 warps/inch, 20 wefts/inch

Pictorial Weavings

40

Pictorial blanket/rug, c. 1880s

Tapestry weave, interlocked, diagonal and eccentric
72 x 51 inches; 8 warps/inch, 38 wefts/inch

41

Pictorial rug, c. 1920

Tapestry weave, interlocked
58 x 33 inches; 8 warps/inch, 32 wefts/inch

Checklist of the Exhibition

Except for the first two dresses which are Pueblo, all other textiles are Navajo.

Dresses and Child's Blanket

1
Pueblo woman's dress, blue borders pattern
c. 1870s
Balanced diamond and diagonal twill weaves
Warp & weft: handspun wool, natural black, blue indigo dye
Stitching: commercial 4-ply wool yarn
Warp & weft selvedges: 3-strand twining, 2-ply cords
40 x 42 inches; 26 warps/inch, 28 wefts/inch

2
Pueblo woman's dress, floral embroidery
c. 1900
Balanced diamond and diagonal twill weaves
Warp & weft: handspun wool, natural brown, blue indigo top-dye
Embroidery: commercial 4-ply wool yarn, aniline dyes
Warp & weft selvedges: 3-strand twining, 2-ply cords
38 x 24 inches; 20 warps/inch, 24 wefts/inch

3
Woman's two-piece dress (Navajo: *biil*)
c. 1860-75
Tapestry weave, interlocked
Warp: handspun wool
Weft: handspun wool, natural black, blue indigo dye; raveled wool yarn, red cochineal and/or lac dye
Warp selvedges: 3-strand twining, 3-ply cords
Weft selvedges: 3-strand twining, 2-ply cords
51 1/2 x 35 inches; 16 warps/inch, 80 wefts/inch

4
Woman's shawl (Spanish: *manta*)
c. 1875
Weft-faced diagonal twill weave
Warp: commercial 4-ply wool yarn
Weft: handspun wool, blue indigo dyes; commercial 4-ply wool yarn, red aniline dye
Warp & weft selvedges: 2-strand twining, 3-ply cords
41 x 52 inches; 12 warps/inch, 42 wefts/inch

5
Child's wearing blanket, classic sarape style
c. 1850-60
Tapestry weave, interlocked
Warp: handspun wool
Weft: handspun wool, natural white, blue indigo dye; raveled wool yarns, untested red dyes; commercial 3-ply wool yarn, red cochineal and/or lac dye
Warp & weft selvedges: 2-strand twining, 3-ply cords
46 x 29 inches; 9 warps/inch, 52 wefts/inch

Chiefs' Blankets

6
Chief's blanket, 1st phase
c. 1870
Weft-faced plain weave
Warp: handspun wool
Weft: handspun wool, natural white, vegetal black top-dye, blue indigo dye; raveled wool yarn, untested red dye
Warp & weft selvedges: 2-strand twining, 2-ply cords
53 x 67 inches; 7 warps/inch, 26-40 wefts/inch

7
Chief's blanket, 2nd phase
c. 1870s
Tapestry weave, dovetailed
Warp: handspun wool
Weft: handspun wool, natural white, brown & gray, blue indigo dye; raveled wool yarn, untested red dyes; commercial 4-ply wool yarn, red aniline dye
Warp & weft selvedges: 2-strand twining, 3-ply cords
53 x 67 inches; 7 warps/inch, 40-50 wefts/inch

8
Chief's blanket, 3rd phase
c. 1870s
Tapestry weave, interlocked
Warp: handspun wool
Weft: handspun wool, natural white & brown, blue indigo dye, vegetal & indigo green top-dye; raveled wool yarn, untested red dye
Warp selvedges: 2-strand twining, 3-ply cords
Weft selvedges: 2-strand twining, 2-ply cords
56 x 75 inches; 9 warps/inch, 40 wefts/inch

9
Chief's blanket, 3rd phase
c. 1870s
Tapestry weave, interlocked
Warp: handspun wool
Weft: handspun wool, natural white, black top-dye, blue indigo dye; raveled wool yarn, untested red dye
Warp selvedges: 3-strand twining, 3-ply cords
Weft selvedges: 2-strand twining, 2-ply cords
54 x 69 inches; 8 inches/warp, 48 wefts/inch

10
Chief's blanket, 3rd phase
c. 1870s
Tapestry weave, interlocked
Warp: handspun wool
Weft: handspun wool, natural white & brown, blue indigo dye; raveled wool yarn, untested red dye; commercial 3-ply wool yarn, untested red dye
Warp & weft selvedges: repaired/replaced
54 x 78 inches; 8 warps/inch, 40-50 wefts/inch

11
Woman's blanket, chief's blanket pattern
c. 1880s
Tapestry weave, interlocked
Warp: handspun wool
Weft: handspun wool, natural white, brown & gray, red aniline dye; raveled wool yarn, untested red & pink dyes
Warp & weft selvedges: 2-strand twining, 4-unplied cords
42 x 50 inches; 8 warps/inch, 36 wefts/inch

12
Woman's blanket, chief's blanket pattern, 2nd phase
c. 1880-85
Tapestry weave, interlocked
Warp & weft: handspun wool, natural white & gray, black top-dye, red aniline dye
Warp selvedges: 2-strand twining, 3-ply cords
Weft selvedges: 2-strand twining, 2-ply cords
44 x 65 inches; 10 warps/inch, 40-46 wefts/inch

13
Transitional blanket/rug, chief's variant
c. 1890
Tapestry weave, interlocked
Warp: handspun wool
Weft: handspun wool, red & orange aniline dye, natural white, brown-black top-dye; commercial 3-ply wool yarn, blue, green & purple aniline dye
Warp selvedges: 2-strand twining, 3-ply cords
Warp selvedges: 2-strand twining, 2-ply cords
61 x 72 inches; 6 warps/inch, 38 wefts/inch

Moqui Stripe Wearing Blankets

14
Wearing blanket, Moqui stripe pattern, 1st phase
c. 1860-70s
Weft-faced plain weave
Warp & weft: handspun wool, natural white & brown, blue indigo dye
Warp selvedges: 2-strand twining, 3-ply cords
Weft selvedges: 2-strand twining, 2-ply cords
77 x 54 inches; 8 warps/inch, 30 wefts/inch

15
Wearing blanket, Moqui stripe pattern
c. 1880
Weft-faced plain weave
Warp: handspun wool
Weft: handspun wool, blue indigo dye, vegetal-on-indigo green top-dye, unknown yellow dye, black top-dye, red aniline dye; raveled wool yarn, red aniline dye
Warp & weft selvedges: 2-strand twining, 3-ply cords
71 x 53 inches; 9 warps/inch, 60 wefts/inch

16
Wearing blanket, Moqui stripe pattern, 3rd phase
c. 1880
Tapestry weave, interlocked
Warp & weft: handspun wool, natural white, black top-dye, blue indigo dye; raveled wool yarn, red aniline dye
Warp & weft selvedges: 2-strand twining, 2-ply cords
74 x 50 inches; 11 warps/inch, 56 wefts/inch

17
Wearing blanket, Moqui stripe pattern
c. 1870s
Tapestry weave, diagonal
Warp & weft: handspun wool, natural white & black, blue indigo dye, red aniline, vegetal-on-indigo green top-dye; commercial red 4-ply in cords
Warp selvedges: worn
Weft selvedges: 2-strand twining, 2-ply cords
78 x 50 inches; 8 warps/inch, 30 wefts/inch

Transitional Blankets

18
Wearing blanket, sarape style
c. 1880s
Tapestry weave, dovetailed
Warp & weft: handspun wool, red & orange aniline dyes, natural white, blue indigo dye, vegetal-on-indigo green top-dye
Warp selvedges: 2-strand twining, 3-ply cords
Weft selvedges: 2-strand twining, 2-ply cords
74 x 52 inches; 11 warps/inch, 44 wefts/inch

19
Transitional blanket
c. 1870
Tapestry weave, dovetailed and diagonal
Warp: handspun wool
Weft: handspun wool, blue indigo; raveled wool yarns, untested red dyes, vegetal yellow dye; commercial 3- & 4-ply wool yarn, natural white, purple & red aniline dyes, unknown yellow dye
Warp & weft selvedges: 2-strand twining, 3-ply cords
75 x 50 inches; 9 warps/inch, 53 wefts/inch

20
Transitional blanket, eye dazzler style
c. 1880
Tapestry weave, interlocked and diagonal
Warp: handspun wool
Weft: handspun wool, blue indigo dye, red aniline dye, natural white; commercial 4-ply wool yarn, unknown yellow and green dyes
Warp selvedges: 3-strand twining, 2-ply cords
Weft selvedges: 2-strand twining, 2-ply cords
82 x 60 inches; 10 warps/inch, 56 wefts/inch

Saddle Blankets/Small Rugs

21
Transitional rug/double saddle blanket, Germantown yarns
c. 1885
Tapestry weave, interlocked
Warp: handspun wool
Weft: commercial 4-ply wool yarn, red, green, yellow, purple, light green aniline dyes
Warp selvedges: 3-strand twining, 2-ply cords, warp and added fringe on one end
Weft selvedges: 2-strand twining, 3-ply cords
52 x 33 inches; 11 warps/inch, 50 wefts/inch

22
Double saddle blanket
c. 1880s
Twill tapestry weave, interlocked
Warp: commercial 4-ply wool yarn
Weft: handspun wool, red, yellow, green & black aniline dyes, natural gray; commercial 4-ply wool yarn, orange, green, purple, blue & red aniline dyes
Warp selvedges: 3-strand twining, 3-ply cords
Warp selvedges: 2-strand twining, 3-ply cords
48 x 31 inches; 9 warps/inch, 30 wefts/inch

23
Double saddle blanket/small rug
c. 1880s
Twill tapestry weave
Warp & weft: handspun wool, red, orange, purple, black & brown aniline dyes, natural white
Warp & weft selvedges: 2-strand twining, 3-ply cords
57 x 33 inches; 7 warps/inch, 28 wefts/inch

24
Double saddle blanket
c. 1880s
Diamond twill weave and twill tapestry weave, interlocked
Warp: commercial 4-ply cotton string
Weft: handspun wool, natural white, red, orange & yellow aniline dyes; commercial 4-ply wool yarn, red, purple, yellow, pink & blue aniline dyes
Warp selvedges: 3-strand twining, 2-ply cords
Warp selvedges: mended
49 x 30 inches; 16 warps/inch, 48-60 wefts/inch

25
Double saddle blanket/small rug
c. 1880s
Twill tapestry weave
Warp & weft: handspun wool, purple, red, green, yellow, magenta, blue & green aniline dyes
Warp & weft selvedges: 2-strand twining, 3-ply cords
53 x 31 inches; 11 warps/inch, 40 wefts/inch

Hubbell Revival Style

26
Transitional blanket/rug, woman's shawl pattern
c. 1890s
Twill tapestry weave, interlocked and dovetailed
Warp & weft: commercial 4-ply wool yarn, natural white, red, purple & yellow aniline dyes
Warp & weft selvedges: 2-strand twining, 3-ply cords
47 x 64 inches; 11 warps/inch, 52 wefts/inch

27
Transitional blanket/rug, woman's shawl pattern
c. 1890s
Tapestry weave, dovetailed
Warp & weft: commercial 4-ply wool yarn, black, purple & red aniline dyes
Warp selvedges: 2-strand twining, 3-ply cords
Warp selvedges: 2-strand twining, 2-ply cords
56 x 66 inches; 9 warps/inch, 40 wefts/inch

28
Transitional blanket/rug, woman's two-piece dress pattern
c. 1890s
Tapestry weave, interlocked
Warp: commercial 4-ply cotton string
Weft: commercial 4-ply wool yarn, green, red & black aniline dyes
Warp selvedges: 2-strand twining, 3-ply cords
Warp selvedges: 2-strand twining, 2-ply cords
51 x 31 inches; 10 warps/inch, 48 wefts/inch

29
Transitional blanket/rug, chief's blanket pattern, 3rd phase variant
c.1890s
Tapestry weave, interlocked
Warp & weft: commercial 4-ply wool yarn, natural white, purple, black & red aniline dyes
Warp selvedges: 2-strand twining, 3-ply cords
Warp selvedges: 2-strand twining, 2-ply cords
66 x 52 inches; 10 warps/inch, 50 wefts/inch

30
Transitional blanket/rug, Moqui stripe pattern
c. 1900
Tapestry weave, dovetailed
Warp: commercial 4-ply wool yarn
Weft: commercial single-ply wool carpet yarn, red, blue & black aniline dyes, natural white; commercial 4-ply wool yarn, red & black aniline dyes
Warp & weft selvedges: 3-strand twining, 3-ply cords
51 x 57 inches; 8 warps/inch, 32 wefts/inch

31
Transitional blanket/rug, Moqui stripe pattern
c. 1890s
Tapestry weave, interlocked
Warp & weft: commercial 4-ply wool yarn, red, purple & black aniline dyes, natural white
Warp selvedges: 3-strand twining, 3-ply cords
Warp selvedges: 2-strand twining, 3-ply cords
70 x 53 inches; 8 warps/inch, 36 wefts/inch

32
Transitional blanket/rug, Moqui stripe pattern
c. 1890s
Tapestry weave, dovetailed
Warp: commercial 4-ply wool yarn
Weft: commercial single-ply wool yarn
Warp selvedges: 3-strand twining, 2-ply cords
Warp selvedges: 2-strand twining, 2-ply cords
77 x 62 inches; 8 warps/inch, 32 wefts/inch

33
Transitional rug
c. 1900-10
Tapestry weave, dovetailed
Warp & weft: commercial 4-ply wool carpet yarn, red and bronze-brown aniline dyes
Selvedges: 2-strand twining, 3-ply cords
86 1/2 x 51 1/2 inches; 9 warps/inch, 42 wefts/inch

34
Transitional blanket, woman's chief-style pattern, variant
c. 1890s
Tapestry weave, diagonal
Warp & weft: handspun wool, red, orange, green, blue & black aniline dyes, natural white
Selvedges: 2-strand twining, 2-ply cords
55 x 68 inches; 6 warps/inch, 18 wefts/inch

35
Pound blanket, woman's chief-style pattern, 2nd phase
c. 1880s
Tapestry weave, interlocked
Warp & weft: handspun wool, red aniline dye, blue indigo dye, black top-dye, natural gray-brown
Warp selvedges: 2-strand twining, 3-ply cords
Weft selvedges: 2-strand twining, 2-ply cords
50 x 67 inches; 7 warps/inch, 40 wefts/inch

36
Pound blanket, woman's or chief's blanket pattern, 3rd phase
c. 1900
Tapestry weave, interlocked
Warp & weft: handspun wool, red, purple & brown aniline dyes, natural white & gray, black top-dye
Selvedges: 2-strand twining, 2-ply cords
57 x 59 1/2 inches; 6 warps/inch, 18-26 wefts/inch

37
Pound blanket, woman's chief-style variant
c. 1890s
Tapestry weave, dovetailed
Warp: commercial 4-ply cotton string
Weft: handspun wool, red, magenta, orange, yellow, purple & gray aniline dyes, natural white, combed gray
Warp selvedges: 2-strand twining, 3-ply cords
Weft selvedges: 2-strand twining, 2-ply cords
36 1/2 x 53 inches; 5 warps/inch, 12 wefts/inch

38
Pound blanket
c. 1880s
Tapestry weave
Warp: commercial 4-ply cotton string
Weft: handspun wool, red, purple, grown, gray and orange aniline dyes, natural white
Selvedges: worn, repaired
85 x 64 inches; 5 warps/inch, 16 wefts/inch

39
Pound blanket, eye dazzler style
c. 1880s
Tapestry weave, dovetailed
Warp: commercial 4-ply cotton string
Weft: handspun wool, aniline dyes, natural white
Selvedges: 2-strand twining, 2-ply cords
72 x 53 inches; 7 warps/inch, 20 wefts/inch

Pictorial Rugs

40
Pictorial blanket/rug, horses
c. 1880s
Tapestry weave, interlocked
Warp & weft: handspun wool, pink & red aniline dye, natural white, brown-black top-dye
Warp selvedges: 2-strand twining, 3-ply cords
Weft selvedges: 2-strand twining, 2-ply cords
72 x 51 inches; 8 warps/inch, 38 wefts/inch

41
Pictorial rug, airplane
c. 1920
Tapestry weave, interlocked
Warp & weft: handspun wool, natural white & brown, brown aniline dye
Warp selvedges: 2-strand twining, 2-ply cords
Weft selvedges: 2-strand twining, single-ply cords
58 x 33 inches; 8 warps/inch, 32 wefts/inch

Not Illustrated:

42
Transitional blanket
c. 1880s
Tapestry weave, interlocked and diagonal
Warp: handspun wool
Weft: handspun wool, red & orange aniline dyes, untested green dye, natural white; commercial 4-ply wool yarn, purple & green aniline dyes
Warp & weft selvedges: 2-strand twining, 3-ply cords
73 x 51 1/2 inches; 9 warps/inch, 30 wefts/inch

43
Saddle blanket/saddle cover
c. 1875-80
Tapestry weave, diagonal
Warp & weft: handspun wool, natural white, blue indigo dye, red aniline dye, vegetal-on-indigo green top-dye; 3- and 4-ply commercial wool yarns, untested green, gold, yellow & red dyes
Warp selvedges: 2-strand twining, 2-ply cords; warp fringe on one end
Weft selvedges: 2-strand twining, 2-ply cords
27 x 34 inches; 10 warps/inch, 36 wefts/inch

44
Transitional blanket/rug, chief's blanket pattern, variant phase
c. 1890s
Tapestry weave, interlocked
Warp: commercial 4-ply cotton string
Weft: handspun wool, red, blue, orange & purple aniline dyes, natural white & brown
Warp selvedges: 2-strand twining, 3-ply cords
Warp selvedges: 2-strand twining, 2-ply cords
58 x 62 inches; 7 warps/inch, 30 wefts/inch

45
Transitional blanket/rug, chief's blanket pattern, variant phase
c. 1890s
Tapestry weave, interlocked
Warp: commercial 4-ply cotton string
Weft: handspun wool, red, blue, yellow & brown aniline dyes, natural brown and white
Selvedges: 2-strand twining, 2-ply cords
57 x 74 inches; 7 warps/inch, 36 wefts/inch

46
Transitional bed blanket (Navajo: *diyogi*)
c. 1880s
Tapestry weave
Warp & weft: handspun wool, natural white & gray, bronze, pink & orange aniline dyes
Warp selvedges: 2-strand twining, 2-ply cords
Weft selvedges: 2-strand twining, 3-ply cords
79 x 52 inches; 6 warps/inch, 14 wefts/inch

47
Pound blanket
c. 1880s
Tapestry weave, dovetailed
Warp & weft: handspun wool, red, green & orange aniline dye, natural white
Selvedges: 2-strand twining, 2-ply cords
56 x 40 inches; 6 warps/inch, 18 wefts/inch

48
Early rug, Moore or Hubbell influence
c. 1900
Tapestry weave, interlocked
Selvedges: 2-strand twining, 2-ply cords
Warp & weft: handspun wool, red aniline dye, black top-dye, natural white
77 x 49 inches; 6 warps/inch, 18 wefts/inch

49
Pound blanket, eye dazzler style
c. 1880s
Tapestry weave
Warp: commercial cotton string
Weft: handspun wool, aniline dyes, natural white
Selvedges: 2-strand twining, 3-ply cords
86 x 55 inches; 6 warps/inch, 16 wefts/inch

50
Early rug, terraced basketry pattern
c. 1900-1925
Tapestry weave, interlocked
Warp & weft: handspun wool, natural white, natural or dyed brown
Warp selvedges: 2-strand twining, 3-ply cords
Weft selvedges: 2-strand twining, 2-ply cords
57 x 38 inches; 7 warps/inch, 26 wefts/inch

BIBLIOGRAPHY

Anderson, Benedict
1991 Imagined Communities: Reflections on the Origin and Spread of Nationalism. New York: Verso.

Benavides, Alonso de
1945 Fray Alonso de Benavides' Revised Memorial of 1634. Frederick W. Hodge, George P. Hammond, and Agapito Rey, eds. Albuquerque: University of New Mexico Press.

Berlant, Anthony, and Mary Hunt Kahlenberg
1977 Walk in Beauty: The Navajo and Their Blankets. Boston: New York Graphic Society.

Blomberg, Nancy J.
1988 Navajo Textiles: The William Randolph Hearst Collection. Tucson: University of Arizona Press.

Blue, Martha
1986 A View from the Bullpen: A Navajo Ken of Traders and Trading Posts. Plateau 57(3):10-17. Flagstaff: Museum of Northern Arizona.

Brody, J.J.
1976 Between Traditions: Navajo Weaving Toward the End of the Nineteenth Century. Iowa City: University of Iowa Museum of Art.

Brugge, David M.
1983 Navajo Prehistory and History to 1850. IN Handbook of North American Indians, Volume 10, Southwest, pp. 489-501. Washington, DC: Smithsonian Institution.

1993 Hubbell Trading Post National Historic Site. Tucson: Southwest Parks and Monuments Association.

Emery, Irene
1966 The Primary Structures of Fabrics. Washington, DC: The Textile Museum.

Farella, John R.
1984 The Main Stalk: A Synthesis of Navajo Philosophy. Tucson: University of Arizona Press.

Hedlund, Ann Lane
1989 Beyond the Loom: Keys to Understanding Early Southwestern Weaving. Boulder: Johnson Publishing for the University of Colorado Museum.

1996 "More of Survival than an Art": Comparing Late Nineteenth- and Late Twentieth-Century Lifeways and Weaving. In Woven by the Grandmothers: Nineteenth-Century Navajo Textiles from the National Museum of the American Indian, edited by Eulalie Bonar, pp. 47-67. Washington, DC: Smithsonian Institution Press.

Hibben, Frank C.
1975 Kiva Art of the Anasazi at Pottery Mound. Las Vegas: KC Publications.

Hobsbawm, Eric, and Terence Ranger, eds.
1983 The Invention of Tradition. Cambridge: Cambridge University Press.

Howard, Kathleen L., and Diana F. Pardue
1996 Inventing the Southwest: The Fred Harvey Company and Native American Art. Flagstaff: Northland Press.

Kent, Kate Peck
1983a Prehistoric Textiles of the Southwest. Santa Fe: School of American Research.

1983b Pueblo Indian Textiles: A Living Tradition. Santa Fe: School of American Research Press.

1985 Navajo Weaving: Three Centuries of Change. Santa Fe: School of American Research Press.

M'Closkey, Kathy
1993 Marketing Multiple Myths: The Hidden History of Navajo Weaving. Journal of the Southwest 36:185-220.

Perez de Luxan, Diego
1929 Expedition into New Mexico Made by Antonio de Espejo, 1582-1583, as Revealed in the Journal of Diego Perez de Luxan, a Member of the Party. George P. Hammond and Agapito Rey, eds., Los Angeles: The Quivira Society.

Reichard, Gladys
1934 Spider Woman: A Story of Navajo Weavers and Chanters. New York: MacMillan. (Reprinted by University of New Mexico Press, 1997).

Ricks, J. Brent, and Alexander E. Anthony, Jr., eds.
1986 The Navajo [a reprint of a catalogue published by J. B. Moore, Indian Trader, of the Crystal Trading Post, New Mexico, in 1911]. Albuquerque: Avanyu Publishing Inc.

Rodee, Marian E.
1981 Old Navajo Rugs: Their Development from 1900 to 1940. Albuquerque: University of New Mexico Press.

Vogt, Evon
1961 Chapter 5: Navaho. In Perspectives on American Indian Culture Change, edited by Edward H. Spicer, pp. 278-336. Chicago: University of Chicago Press.

Webster, Laurie D.
1996 Reproducing the Past: Revival and Revision in Navajo Weaving. Journal of the Southwest 38(4):415-431.

Wheat, Joe Ben
1984 The Gift of Spiderwoman: Southwestern Textiles, The Navajo Tradition. Philadelphia: The University Museum, University of Pennsylvania.

1985 Navajo Basketry. Paper presented at the biennial meeting of the Native American Art Studies Association, Denver.

1988 Early Trade and Commerce in Southwestern Textiles before the Curio Shop. In Reflections: Papers on Southwestern Culture History in Honor of Charles H. Lange, edited by Anne V. Poore, pp. 57-72. Papers of the Archaeological Society of New Mexico No. 14. Santa Fe.

Wheat, Joe Ben, and Lucy Fowler Williams
1994 A Burst of Brilliance: Germantown and Navajo Weaving. Philadelphia: University of Pennsylvania.